NIACIN EDUCATORS

BORROWED CLARITY

Why Smart Founders Are Still Making Financial Decisions in the Dark

BY

REHANA MOHAMMED

TABLE OF CONTENTS

Introduction 1

Act I: The Illusion 5

Chapter 1: The Illusion of Progress 7
Chapter 2: Revenue Is Not Relief 11
Chapter 3: The Bank Balance Lie 15
Chapter 4: Why Smart People Stay Stuck 19

Act II: The Reframe 23

Chapter 5: This Isn't a Money Problem 25
Chapter 6: Financial Stress Is a Signal 29
Chapter 7: Cognitive Load Is Expensive 33
Chapter 8: Growth Can Create Pressure 37
Chapter 9: The Borrowed Clarity Problem 41

Act III: The System 45

Chapter 10: Revenue Reality 47
Chapter 11: Founder Pay Alignment 51
Chapter 12: Cost Structure Awareness 55
Chapter 13: Decision Timing 59
Chapter 14: Integration 63

Act IV: The Transformation 67

Chapter 15: Financial Range of Motion 69
Chapter 16: The New Standard 73
Chapter 17: Clarity Before Crisis 79
Chapter 18: You Were Never Bad With Money 83
Chapter 19: The Decision You Make Now 87
Closing: An Invitation 91

INTRODUCTION

I didn't learn about money in a classroom.

I learned it in tension.

Growing up, money was always present in my house, but not always stable. There were seasons where things felt abundant. Seasons where everything tightened. Same people. Same work ethic. Different outcomes.

What changed wasn't effort.

It was how decisions were being made under pressure.

I didn't have language for that then. I just watched. I watched the way financial uncertainty quietly shaped everything; not just what we could afford, but how people moved through the day. Whether they felt confident or cautious. Whether decisions felt like choices or like risks.

Years later, I walked into the professional world expecting clarity. I had the credentials. I had the experience. I had spent years inside Big 4 firms, industry roles, consulting rooms and boardrooms; places where numbers were supposed to mean something definitive.

But what I found, inside businesses and inside conversations with founders, was the same pattern I had seen growing up.

People making money. Without understanding what it meant.

Not because they weren't intelligent. Not because they weren't working hard. But because the information available to them had never been translated into something they could actually use to make decisions.

They had revenue. They had reports. They had advisors explaining what everything meant.

And they were still operating in the dark.

That realization changed everything for me. Because once I saw it, I couldn't unsee it.

* * *

Here is what I have learned after more than sixteen years working inside financial systems, consulting with founders and sitting across from women who were building real businesses while quietly carrying the weight of not fully understanding what their money was doing:

The problem is never the money.

The problem is the decision-making that happens or doesn't happen because of a lack of clarity around what the money means.

That's the thesis of this book. And it has two parts that most financial conversations never address simultaneously.

The first part is the cost of avoidance. When founders don't engage with their numbers, when they delay, defer, or disconnect from their financial picture, the risk doesn't disappear. It compounds. Quietly. Invisibly. Until it isn't quiet or invisible anymore.

The second part is more sophisticated and it is the reason I wrote this book.

You can avoid avoidance entirely. You can hire the CPA, engage the bookkeeper, bring on the fractional CFO. You can sit in every meeting, review every report and nod along to every recommendation. And you can still be financially vulnerable, because you never developed the lens to evaluate what you're being told.

That is borrowed clarity.

Borrowed clarity is what happens when you outsource not just the execution of your finances, but the interpretation of them. When the explanations you receive feel logical enough that you adopt them without fully understanding them. When your financial confidence depends on another person being in the room.

It feels like clarity.

It is not ownership.

And the difference between those two things determines everything about how you make decisions, how you lead your business and how protected you are when circumstances change and the advisor is no longer there to explain what's happening.

*　*　*

This book is not for founders who are failing.

It is for founders who are succeeding and still feel like something is off. Who have built real businesses, generated real revenue, hired real professionals and yet cannot fully answer the question: what is my money actually doing?

It is for the founder who opened her bank account after crossing a milestone she had been chasing for years and felt hesitation instead of relief.

It is for the founder who reviews every report her CPA sends and thinks: this sounds right, without being able to explain why.

It is for the founder who is done operating on someone else's interpretation of her own business.

What follows is not a financial literacy course. I am not here to teach you accounting. I am not here to make you a numbers person, because that framing misses the point entirely.

I am here to give you a decision system. A lens that belongs to you. One that doesn't disappear when the meeting ends, when the advisor leaves, or when the report stops making sense.

The Niacin Clarity Framework, built around the five financial decisions that determine whether your revenue actually improves your life, is that system.

But before we get there, we have to dismantle what you've been taught to believe.

We have to look honestly at the illusion of progress. At the myth that more revenue is the solution. At the false security of a clean bank balance and a trusted advisor who seems to have everything under control.

And then, once the real problem is visible, we build something better.

Something that is yours.

* * *

One more thing before you turn the page.

You were never bad with money.

You were working without the right lens. You were making decisions with incomplete translation. You were operating inside a system that was designed to be understood by professionals, not by the founders it was supposed to serve.

That changes now.

Not because you are going to become a different person.

Because you are going to take back what was always yours to own.

Act I

THE ILLUSION

CHAPTER 1

The Illusion of Progress

You can make more money this year and feel worse than you did last year.

I've sat in rooms with founders who were doing everything right, at least on paper.

Revenue was up. Clients were coming in. The business looked like it was growing. From the outside, it was working.

But the conversations didn't match the numbers.

They weren't talking about expansion. They weren't talking about vision. They were asking questions that didn't make sense for someone who was supposedly growing.

"Why does it feel like there's never enough left over?"

"Where is the money actually going?"

"Can I even afford to hire?"

And the one that always stayed with me: "If the business is doing well, why doesn't it feel like it?"

I remember sitting across from one founder in particular. She had just crossed a revenue milestone she had been chasing for years. The kind people celebrate publicly. The kind that looks like proof that things are working.

But instead of excitement, there was hesitation. She was slower to make decisions. More cautious with spending. Second-guessing things she used to feel confident about.

At one point she paused and said: "I thought getting here would feel different."

That sentence told me everything. Because I had heard it before. Different industry. Different business. Same feeling.

And it wasn't just happening in those rooms. I had seen a version of this long before I ever worked with a client.

Growing up, money was always present in my house, but not always stable. There were seasons where things felt abundant. And seasons where everything tightened. The same people. The same work ethic. Different outcomes.

What changed wasn't effort. It was how decisions were being made under pressure.

I didn't have language for it then. But sitting in those rooms years later, listening to founders ask the same questions in different ways, it became impossible to ignore.

There was a pattern. People weren't confused because they lacked intelligence. They were confused because the numbers they were looking at didn't match the reality they were living.

—

Most people believe progress in business is obvious. You make more money. Things get easier. More revenue should mean more stability, more confidence, more freedom.

So when those things don't happen, the assumption is: "I need to make more."

But that assumption hides something dangerous. Because if more money actually solved the problem, you wouldn't still feel this way.

The blind spot is this: you're measuring progress by input, not by what that input actually produces.

Revenue is being treated like a result. But it's not. It's just the starting point.

* * *

Revenue doesn't create clarity. It amplifies whatever already exists.

If your financial structure is unclear at $100K, it will be more unclear at $300K. If your decisions are reactive at one level, they become more expensive at the next. Growth doesn't fix misalignment. It exposes it.

That's why so many founders feel a quiet tension as their business grows. Not because something is wrong. But because something hasn't been translated yet.

The numbers are moving. But they don't mean anything useful. And when numbers don't translate, decisions become guesses.

* * *

This is the shift that changes everything: Revenue is not progress. Clarity is.

Progress is not how much comes in. Not how busy you are. Not how fast you're growing. Progress is knowing what your business actually produces. Understanding what you can afford to do next. Being able to make decisions without hesitation.

This is where most people get stuck. Because they skip the step that makes everything else work: translation.

Revenue becomes profit. Profit becomes owner pay. Owner pay becomes stability. Stability becomes the foundation for decision-making.

Without that translation, revenue is just noise. And noise creates pressure.

* * *

You are not someone who needs to make more money to feel in control.

You are someone who needs to understand what your money is already doing.

There's a difference. One keeps you chasing. The other puts you in position.

The moment you stop asking "how do I make more?" and start asking "what is this actually producing?", everything changes. Because now you're not reacting to your business. You're reading it.

* * *

You don't have a growth problem.

You have a clarity problem.

And until that changes, more will never feel like enough.

CHAPTER 2

Revenue Is Not Relief

Revenue doesn't solve financial stress. In many cases, it creates it.

There's a moment I've seen happen more times than I can count.

A founder hits a new level of revenue. It might be their first $10K month. Or their first $50K month. Or a year that finally crosses into multiple six figures. On paper, it's a breakthrough. The kind of milestone that's supposed to signal: you made it.

And for a moment, it does feel like that. There's excitement. Momentum. A sense that things are finally working.

But then something subtle starts to shift.

Expenses begin to rise. Not dramatically at first, but enough to go unnoticed. A new tool here. A contractor there. More ad spend. More software. More support. Because growth requires support. And support costs money.

At the same time, expectations increase. The business needs to maintain this level. Clients expect more. Delivery expands. Complexity grows.

And then the moment comes. They log into their bank account expecting to feel a sense of relief. And instead, there's hesitation. The number is higher than it used to be. But it doesn't feel like more. It feels allocated. Already spoken for. Already committed. Already gone.

And that's when the questions start again.

"Why does it still feel tight?"

"Where is it all going?"

"How am I making more, but not keeping more?"

I've watched founders try to solve that feeling the only way they know how. They push for more. More clients. More offers. More revenue streams. Because logically, that should fix it.

But instead of relief, they feel heavier. More responsibility. More moving parts. More pressure to maintain. And the original problem? Still there. Just buried under more money.

* * *

Most founders believe revenue is the solution.

If things feel tight: make more. If things feel unclear: make more. If things feel unstable: make more. Revenue becomes the answer to everything.

But that belief creates a cycle that's hard to see while you're in it. Because every time pressure shows up, you respond with expansion. And expansion without clarity multiplies the pressure.

The blind spot is this: you are using revenue to solve problems that revenue was never designed to fix.

* * *

Revenue is not relief. Revenue is responsibility.

Every dollar that enters your business comes with a decision attached to it. Where it goes. What it supports. What it enables. What it requires you to sustain.

And if those decisions aren't clear, revenue doesn't feel like freedom. It feels like weight.

That's why so many founders hit higher income levels and feel more stressed instead of less. Because they didn't just increase revenue. They increased financial complexity, operational demands and decision volume, without increasing clarity.

And clarity is the only thing that turns money into something usable.

* * *

Money only feels like relief when it has a defined role.

Undefined money creates tension. Defined money creates control.

This is where your financial structure matters. Every dollar needs a job before it arrives, or at least immediately after. Not in theory. In structure.

Revenue must be intentionally distributed: into what the business needs to operate, what the owner is paid, what is reserved for taxes and what is retained for stability.

Without that structure, revenue sits in one place and creates confusion. Because you're constantly asking: "Can I afford this?" And the real answer is: you don't know. Not because you're incapable. Because the money hasn't been assigned meaning yet.

* * *

You are not someone waiting for revenue to fix your business.

You are someone who assigns purpose to the money your business generates.

That's the difference between reacting and leading. Reactive founders chase income. Strategic founders define it.

The moment you stop treating revenue like relief and start treating it like a resource to be directed, you step into a different role. Not just someone who earns money. But someone who controls what it does.

* * *

Revenue doesn't change your business.

What you do with it does.

CHAPTER 3

The Bank Balance Lie

| *Your bank balance is not telling you the truth.*

I can usually tell how a founder is making decisions within the first few minutes of a conversation. Not by what they say. By how they answer one question:

"Can you afford to make that decision right now?"

If there's a pause. If they hesitate. If they say "I think so" or "It looks like it", I already know what they're using. They're looking at their bank account. And trying to make a decision from a number that has no context.

I've seen founders with six figures in their account delay hiring someone they needed months ago. I've also seen founders with far less commit to expenses that put them in a position they couldn't sustain.

Same tool. Different outcomes. Because the issue isn't the number. It's what they think the number means.

* * *

Most founders use their bank balance as their primary decision-making tool. It feels logical. Money is either there, or it isn't.

So the thinking becomes: "If the money is in the account, I can afford it." "If the account feels low, I need to slow down." Simple. Immediate. And completely misleading.

Because your bank balance is not a decision tool. It's a snapshot. It shows you what exists in one moment, but tells you nothing about what's already committed, what's about to leave, what needs to be reserved, what actually belongs to you.

The blind spot is this: you are treating available cash as available decision space. And those are not the same thing.

* * *

Your bank balance doesn't represent what you have. It represents what hasn't moved yet.

That includes tax obligations you haven't paid, expenses that haven't cleared, payroll that hasn't been processed and money that should never be spent in the first place.

When all of that sits in one account, it creates a false sense of flexibility. And that false sense leads to two types of behavior:

Overconfidence: "This looks like enough, I'll move forward." Or hesitation: "This feels tight, I should wait."

Both are based on incomplete information. Which means both are guesses. And guesses, when repeated, turn into patterns.

* * *

If you're using your bank balance to make decisions, here is what you need to replace it with.

First: separation before interpretation. Money must be separated into categories before it becomes usable. At minimum, operating funds for what the business runs on, owner pay for what you take home, taxes for what is not yours and profit reserves for what creates stability. If everything sits in one account, you don't have clarity. You have a pile.

Second: defined decision pools. Every decision should pull from a specific category, not from "what's available." A hiring decision comes from operating capacity. Personal spending comes from owner pay. Tax payments are already reserved. If you don't know which pool a decision pulls from, you're not making a decision. You're making a guess.

Third: a weekly visibility rhythm. Clarity is not a one-time setup. It's a rhythm. Once a week, you should be able to answer: what did we bring in? Where did it go? What is actually available? What decisions can we confidently make next? If you can't answer those without hesitation, you are still operating from your bank balance.

Fourth: replace "can I afford this?" with "which category does this decision come from and is it supported there?" That one shift changes everything. Because now you're not reacting to a number. You're making a decision inside a structure.

* * *

You are not someone who checks your account to decide what's possible.

You are someone who defines what your money is allowed to do.

That's control. That's leadership. That's clarity. The difference isn't intelligence. It's structure.

And once structure exists, your bank balance stops being a source of anxiety. It becomes what it was always meant to be: a result. Not a guide.

* * *

If your bank balance is making your decisions, you're not in control of your business.

You're reacting to it.

CHAPTER 4

Why Smart People Stay Stuck

> *You are not stuck because you don't understand money. You are stuck because you've never been taught how to interpret it and because somewhere along the way, you stopped asking whether the interpretation you were given was actually yours.*

There's a specific kind of frustration that doesn't get talked about enough.

It doesn't look like failure. From the outside, everything appears to be working. You're capable. You're resourceful. You've figured out things most people haven't. You've built something.

And yet, when it comes to your numbers, there's hesitation. You open the report and skim it. You look at the dashboard and move on. You tell yourself you'll get into it later.

Not because you don't care. But because something about it feels unclear. Heavy. Like you should understand it, but don't fully trust that you do.

So instead, you rely on what does feel clear: your instincts. Your experience. Your ability to figure things out as you go.

And for a while, that works. Until it doesn't. Until decisions start carrying more weight. More risk. More consequence. And suddenly, the place you've been avoiding is the place you need most.

But here is what makes this more complicated than simple avoidance.

Most founders aren't just avoiding their numbers. They're operating on someone else's understanding of them.

A report gets delivered. An explanation is given. A recommendation is made. And it sounds right. So they move forward. Not because they fully understand it, but because someone else did. That's where the disconnect begins. And it's where the real problem lives.

* * *

Most people assume that if something feels confusing, it's because they're not good at it.

So when it comes to money, the internal narrative becomes: "I'm just not a numbers person." "I need someone else to handle this." "I'll focus on what I'm good at."

That belief feels harmless. Even practical. But it creates a subtle pattern: avoid, delegate, disconnect. And over time, that disconnection grows.

Not because you lack intelligence. But because you were never given a way to engage with your numbers that made sense. And because once you started delegating the interpretation, not just the execution, you stopped building the capacity to evaluate what you were being told.

The blind spot is this: you've mistaken lack of translation for lack of capability. And you think you're making informed decisions, when you're actually adopting someone else's interpretation.

* * *

This isn't a knowledge problem. It's a language problem and an ownership problem.

Financial information is often presented in a way that prioritizes accuracy over usability. Reports are structured for compliance. Terminology is designed for professionals. But you're not trying to file a report. You're trying to make decisions.

And decision-making requires something different: clarity. Not more information. Better interpretation and specifically, interpretation that belongs to you.

Because here's what changes when you own the interpretation: you can pressure-test it. You can ask whether it aligns with what you know about your business. You can evaluate a recommendation instead of just accepting it. You can make the final call from understanding, not from trust alone.

Once numbers are translated into meaning that you own, everything changes. Because now you're not looking at data through someone else's lens. You're seeing direction through yours.

* * *

INFORMATION → EXPLANATION → AGREEMENT → ACTION
(No ownership)

VERSUS

INFORMATION → UNDERSTANDING → INTERPRETATION
→ DECISION
(Ownership)

* * *

You are not someone who avoids numbers.

You are someone who hasn't been given a system that makes them usable and who has been quietly handing interpretation to others without realizing what that costs.

Once you have that system, you don't need to become a different person. You become more of who you already are. Capable. Decisive. Clear.

* * *

You don't need to know everything.

But you do need to understand enough to decide.

Act II

THE REFRAME

CHAPTER 5

This Isn't a Money Problem

If more money would fix it, it would have fixed it by now.

There's a question I hear often. It usually comes after someone has walked me through their business. Their revenue. Their offers. Their expenses. Their growth. They explain everything clearly. And then they pause and ask: "So what do you think I need to do?"

They expect the answer to be: make more. More clients. More offers. More volume. Because that's what they've been told. That's what they've been trying.

And on the surface, it makes sense. But what stands out to me is never how little they're making. It's how much is already there, without clarity.

I've had conversations with founders at different levels. Some trying to get to their first consistent month. Others already generating more than they ever thought they would. Different numbers. Same tension. Same questions. Same uncertainty around decisions that should feel clear.

And at some point in the conversation, I'll say something that usually stops them.

"This isn't a money problem."

There's always a pause. Because if it's not money, then what is it?

The real answer has two layers. The first layer is clarity, they don't have a clear picture of what their revenue is actually producing, what their business can support, or what decisions are available to them. But the second layer is the one that changes everything: it's not just that they lack clarity. It's that the clarity they think they have isn't theirs.

They've been told what things mean. They've received explanations that sounded right. They've agreed to recommendations they couldn't fully evaluate. And they've moved forward on borrowed understanding, not their own.

More money doesn't fix that. Better advisors don't fix that. Cleaner reports don't fix that. Because if the interpretation isn't yours, the decision isn't either.

* * *

Most founders have been conditioned to believe that money is the constraint.

If something feels off, the assumption is: not enough revenue. Not enough clients. Not enough scale. So the response becomes: increase income, expand capacity, push harder.

And sometimes, that works temporarily. But it doesn't resolve the underlying tension. Because the problem was never the amount. It was the lack of clarity around what the amount was doing and who was responsible for interpreting it.

The blind spot is this: you are trying to solve a clarity ownership problem with a quantity solution. And quantity without ownership creates complexity.

—

Money is not the problem. Money is the amplifier.

It takes whatever is unclear and makes it harder to ignore. If your structure is unclear, more money means more confusion. If your decisions are reactive, more money means more pressure. If someone else is interpreting what your numbers mean, more money means more dependence on that person to tell you whether you're okay.

That's why growth often feels heavier instead of easier. Because the system underneath the growth hasn't been built to support it. And the interpretation of that system hasn't been claimed by the person it belongs to.

So instead of creating relief, money creates responsibility without direction. And responsibility without direction always feels like stress.

—

Here is what changes everything:

The problem is not how much money you make. The problem is how clearly you can make decisions about it and whether the clarity you're operating from is actually yours.

> *"If your clarity depends on someone else being in the room, it was never yours."*

Can you clearly answer: what is this business actually producing? What can I afford to do next? What needs to change and what doesn't? And when you answer those questions, are you answering them from your own understanding, or from what someone else told you to think?

If the interpretation isn't yours, you don't have decision clarity. You have borrowed confidence. And borrowed confidence disappears the moment the person you borrowed it from isn't in the room.

* * *

You are not a founder trying to make enough money to feel stable.

You are a founder learning how to make clear decisions with the money you already have, from a lens that belongs to you.

That's where control comes from. That's where confidence comes from. That's where growth actually becomes sustainable.

Because once you can make decisions clearly, from your own understanding, you stop chasing more as the solution. And start using what exists as leverage.

* * *

You don't need more money to fix your business.

You need clarity to use it. And you need that clarity to be yours.

CHAPTER 6

Financial Stress Is a Signal

Financial stress doesn't mean something is wrong.
It means something is unclear.

There's a specific kind of pressure that comes with running a business. It doesn't always look like panic. Most of the time, it looks like constant thinking. Low-level tension. A feeling that something needs attention, even when you can't name exactly what.

You're moving through your day. Responding to messages. Delivering work. Showing up for clients. On the surface, everything is functioning.

But underneath, there's a quiet loop running: "Am I okay?" "Are we good?" "Is there something I'm missing?"

You open your bank account more than you need to. Not always because you're about to make a decision. Sometimes just to check. To confirm. To reassure yourself that things are still in place.

And for a moment, it works. Until it doesn't. Because the number doesn't answer the question you're actually asking.

So you keep moving. You tell yourself it's just part of growth. That this level of pressure is normal. That things will settle once you hit the next level. The next revenue goal. The next milestone. The next version of stability.

But even when you reach those moments, the feeling doesn't fully leave. It shifts. Becomes more subtle. More complex. Less about survival. More about responsibility.

"Can I sustain this?" "Can I make the right decisions from here?" "What happens if I get this wrong?"

I've sat with founders in that space. Not in crisis. Not failing. But carrying a level of pressure that didn't match what their business looked like from the outside. And what stood out wasn't the numbers. It was the uncertainty behind them. Because stress doesn't come from numbers alone. It comes from not knowing what they mean.

* * *

Most people treat financial stress as something to eliminate. Something to fix. Something that signals: "I'm behind." "I'm doing something wrong." "I need to work harder."

So the response becomes: push more. Do more. Earn more. Or avoid it altogether. Distract. Delay. Defer. Because stress feels like a problem.

But that interpretation misses something important.

The blind spot is this: you're treating stress like the issue, instead of the information.

* * *

Stress is not random. It's not something that shows up without reason. It's a response. A signal. An indication that something in your environment, or your understanding of it, is incomplete.

Think about where financial stress actually shows up. Not in moments of total clarity. Not when decisions feel obvious. It shows up when you're unsure if you can afford something. When you don't know what's coming next. When you feel responsible for outcomes you can't fully see.

Stress is your system telling you: "There's something here that hasn't been translated yet."

Not: "You're failing." Not: "You're behind." Just: "You don't have full visibility."

And without visibility, everything feels heavier than it actually is.

* * *

If stress is a signal, the question becomes: what is it pointing to?

Most financial stress falls into three categories.

The first is visibility gaps. You don't have a clear picture of what's happening. You're asking: what is actually coming in? What is actually going out? What is left over? When visibility is low, your brain fills in the gaps with uncertainty. And uncertainty creates stress.

The second is allocation confusion. Money exists, but it's not clearly assigned. So every decision feels like it's pulling from the same place. You're asking: can I afford this? Should I wait? Is this responsible? Without defined roles for your money, every decision carries tension.

The third is decision pressure. You are required to make decisions without feeling equipped to make them. Hiring. Spending. Investing. Not because you lack intelligence, but because the information you have doesn't feel usable. So every decision feels like risk. Even when it's not.

Instead of asking "how do I get rid of this stress?", ask: "what is this stress trying to show me?"

Because once you identify the category, you can respond correctly. Visibility gap means increase clarity. Allocation issue means restructure money. Decision pressure means improve interpretation. Stress becomes directional. Not emotional.

* * *

You are not someone who needs to eliminate stress to feel confident.

You are someone who knows how to read it.

That changes your relationship with it completely. Because now, when stress shows up, you don't spiral. You don't avoid. You don't overcorrect. You investigate. You interpret. You adjust.

And that's what creates stability. Not the absence of pressure, but the ability to respond to it with clarity.

* * *

Stress isn't telling you something is wrong.

It's telling you something needs to be understood.

CHAPTER 7

Cognitive Load Is Expensive

The most expensive thing in your business isn't a bad decision. It's the mental weight of not knowing what the right one is.

There's a level of exhaustion that doesn't come from doing too much. It comes from thinking too much.

Not focused thinking. Not strategic thinking. Background thinking. The kind that never fully turns off.

You wake up and it's already there. Before your feet hit the floor, your mind starts scanning: what needs to be done. What hasn't been handled. What might be coming next.

You move through your day, checking things off. Responding. Delivering. Solving. But even in the middle of getting things done, there's a second layer running underneath it all.

A quiet, constant processing loop: "Did I miss anything?" "Can I afford to make that move?" "Should I be doing something differently right now?"

It shows up in small moments. You open your bank account, not to act, but to check. You revisit the same numbers, without new clarity. You delay a decision, not because you don't care, but because you don't feel certain.

And the hardest part? From the outside, everything still looks like it's working. You're producing. You're showing up. You're growing.

But internally, your mental energy is being split. Part of you is executing. The other part is holding uncertainty.

And that split is where the exhaustion comes from.

—

Most people assume their exhaustion is a time problem.

"I just need more hours." "I need to be more efficient." "I need better systems for productivity."

So they optimize their calendars. They restructure their days. They try to become more disciplined. But the fatigue doesn't go away.

Because the issue isn't time. It's cognitive load.

The blind spot is this: you are carrying decisions in your head that should be supported by structure. And anything that lives in your head, has to be processed over and over again.

* * *

Your brain is not designed to hold unresolved decisions indefinitely. It's designed to process, decide and move on.

But when clarity is missing, decisions don't resolve. They linger. They reopen. They repeat. So instead of thinking once and acting, you think multiple times without closure.

That repetition is what creates mental weight. Not the complexity of your business. But the lack of finality in your decisions.

And when that becomes your normal state, it doesn't just affect how you feel. It affects how you operate. Because cognitive load doesn't stay in one place. It shows up in slower decisions, delayed action, second-guessing, reduced confidence.

Not because you've lost capability. Because your capacity is being used to hold uncertainty.

* * *

Every unresolved financial question creates ongoing cognitive cost. And those costs compound.

Most financial cognitive load comes from three sources.

The first is undefined numbers. You have access to information, but not clarity. So you keep revisiting the same data: checking accounts, reviewing reports, scanning dashboards. Without resolution. This creates repetitive thinking without progress.

The second is unmade decisions. There are decisions you know you need to make, but haven't. Hiring. Investing. Adjusting pricing. So they stay open loops. And open loops require energy. Every time your brain returns to them, it spends more.

The third is untrusted systems. Even when systems exist, you don't fully trust them. So instead of relying on structure, you double-check. You override. You re-evaluate. Which puts the responsibility back on you.

Reducing cognitive load is not about thinking less. It's about closing loops through clarity. That means defining what your numbers mean. Assigning roles to your money. Making decisions inside a structure. Trusting the system you've built.

When those things are in place, your brain stops holding everything. Because it doesn't have to.

* * *

You are not someone who needs to work harder to keep up.

You are someone who needs to remove what your mind was never meant to carry.

Because leadership is not about holding more. It's about deciding what gets held and what gets structured.

And once your financial decisions are supported, your mental energy returns to where it belongs. Not managing uncertainty. But leading your business.

* * *

You're not overwhelmed because your business is too much.

You're overwhelmed because too much of it lives in your head.

CHAPTER 8

Growth Can Create Pressure

Growth doesn't always feel like progress.
Sometimes, it feels like pressure.

There's a version of growth that no one really talks about. The kind that looks successful from the outside, but feels heavier from the inside.

It starts the way you expect. More clients. More revenue. More opportunities. Things you worked toward. Things you wanted. And at first, it feels good. Validating. Energizing. Like momentum is finally on your side.

But then something subtle begins to shift.

Your calendar fills faster than it used to. Your time feels more allocated. The margin you once had starts to disappear. Decisions that used to feel simple start requiring more thought. More consideration. More weight.

You notice yourself pausing longer before committing to things. Rechecking numbers. Revisiting plans. Thinking through scenarios that never used to cross your mind.

Not because you're unsure of yourself. But because the stakes feel different now. There's more to maintain. More to protect. More that could be impacted by a single decision.

And then there's the part no one sees. The quiet awareness that growth didn't just increase what's possible, it increased what's required. More responsibility. More expectations. More complexity.

And at some point, a question starts to form: "Why does this feel harder, when things are going better?"

* * *

Most founders believe growth will simplify things. More revenue means more ease. More success means more freedom. More momentum means more stability.

So when the opposite happens, it creates confusion. Because no one prepares you for the reality that growth doesn't reduce complexity. It increases it.

The blind spot is this: you expected growth to remove pressure, without realizing it multiplies what needs to be managed.

* * *

Growth is not just an increase in income. It's an increase in decisions.

Every new level introduces more moving parts, more financial commitments, more variables to consider. And if the structure underneath your business hasn't evolved with that growth, you feel it. Not immediately. But gradually.

In the form of slower decision-making. Increased hesitation. Subtle tension around things that used to feel simple.

It's not that growth is the problem. It's that growth requires a different level of clarity than the one that got you there. And without that shift, what should feel like expansion starts to feel like pressure.

* * *

Every new level of revenue requires a new level of decision clarity.

If clarity doesn't scale with growth, pressure will.

What's actually increasing as you grow isn't just income. It's decision volume: more money means more choices about hiring, investment, pricing and capacity. Without clarity, each decision takes longer and carries more weight.

It's also financial commitments: growth introduces recurring expenses, team obligations and higher operating costs. Which means more of your revenue is already spoken for before you even touch it.

And it's risk sensitivity. At higher levels, mistakes feel different. Not because you're less capable, but because the impact is larger. So your brain compensates by analyzing more, hesitating more, trying to get it right. Which slows you down.

Growth becomes easier when structure increases at the same rate as complexity. That means clearer financial visibility. Defined allocation of money. Faster, supported decision-making. Because the goal isn't to avoid complexity. It's to be equipped for it.

* * *

You are not someone who grows your business and hopes it becomes easier.

You are someone who expands your clarity as your business expands.

That's what allows growth to feel like progress, instead of pressure. Because now, when things increase, your capacity to manage them increases with it. Not through effort. Through structure.

* * *

Growth doesn't create pressure.

Outgrowing your clarity does.

CHAPTER 9

The Borrowed Clarity Problem

> *You don't have a clarity problem. You have an ownership problem.*

I was sitting with a founder who, on paper, was doing everything right.

Strong revenue. Clean books. A CPA she trusted. Nothing looked broken.

We walked through her numbers together. Revenue made sense. Expenses were categorized. Reports were organized.

And yet, when it came time to make a decision, she paused. Not briefly. Noticeably.

I asked a simple question: "What do you think this means?"

She hesitated. Then said: "I think I understand it, but I don't know what I would do differently."

That's the moment it becomes clear. Not when something is wrong. When everything looks right, but the decision still doesn't feel grounded.

From the outside, it looked like clarity. The numbers were there. The reports were clean. The explanations had been given. But internally, there was no ownership. She wasn't deciding from understanding. She was deciding from trust.

And those are not the same thing.

* * *

This is what most people miss: you can feel informed and still not be in control.

Because clarity is not hearing an explanation. It is not receiving a report. It is not agreeing with a recommendation.

Clarity is being able to interpret what you see and decide from it.

* * *

Borrowed clarity is when you're making decisions using financial interpretations you didn't create, don't fully understand and can't confidently challenge.

It feels like clarity. But it's not yours.

Here is what it looks like in practice.

Your CPA says: "We should reinvest to reduce your tax burden." Your CFO says: "This is the most efficient way to grow." A report shows: "You're on track." And you respond: "Okay, that makes sense."

But underneath, you're not pressure-testing it. You're not translating it. You're not aligning it with what you know about your business. You're adopting it.

* * *

Borrowed clarity creates three specific problems.

The first is signal distortion. When you're seeing your business through someone else's lens, you're not getting a clear picture, you're getting their interpretation of the picture. And their interpretation is shaped by their expertise, their assumptions and their priorities. Not yours.

The second is false confidence. You feel informed, but you're not grounded. You can repeat what you've been told. You can nod through the meeting. But if the numbers shift or the situation changes, you don't have the foundation to recalibrate. You have to wait for someone else to tell you what it means.

The third and most damaging, is ownership erosion. Over time, you stop asking "what do I think?" and start asking "what do they recommend?" Your financial decision-making muscle weakens from disuse. And the gap between your business and your understanding of it widens, quietly, until a decision arrives that you cannot delegate and you realize you have no framework of your own to make it.

* * *

This is not because founders are incapable.

It's because no one taught them how to build a decision system.

So when they hire experts, they don't just outsource execution. They outsource interpretation. And eventually, judgment.

The problem isn't that advisors are wrong. The problem is that you don't realize what you've handed over.

* * *

You don't need to become the expert.

But you do need to become the owner of the lens.

That means you understand what matters. You recognize what's noise. You evaluate recommendations against your own understanding of your business. And you make the final call from a position of informed authority, not deference.

I once said this to a founder: "If your advisor left tomorrow, what decisions would you still feel confident making?"

She didn't answer immediately. And that silence said everything.

You are not someone who relies on financial explanations.

You are someone who understands what those explanations mean.

That's the difference between being informed and being in control.

> *"If your clarity disappears when your advisor leaves the room, it was never yours."*

* * *

DATA → ADVISOR INTERPRETATION → FOUNDER AGREEMENT → DECISION

(No Ownership)

Act III

THE SYSTEM

CHAPTER 10

Revenue Reality

> *Revenue is the most celebrated number in business and the least understood.*

I remember sitting across from a founder who had just hit a milestone she had been chasing for years.

It was the kind of number people post about. The kind that gets celebrated. Proof that things are working. She smiled when she said it. But it didn't last long.

Because right after, she leaned forward slightly and lowered her voice.

"Can I ask you something?"

I nodded. She paused.

"If I'm making this much, why doesn't it feel like I have it?"

There was no panic in her voice. Just confusion. A quiet kind of frustration that doesn't come from failure, but from something not adding up.

So I asked her a simple question. "How much of that revenue do you actually take home?"

She blinked. Looked away for a second. Then back at me. "I don't know."

Not because she hadn't thought about it. But because she didn't have a clear answer. And that's the moment where things usually begin. Not when revenue increases. But when someone realizes: they don't know what it means.

I've seen this play out across different levels. A founder trying to get to consistent income, asking why nothing feels stable. Another already generating multiple six figures, still unsure what she can actually afford to do next. Different numbers. Same disconnect.

They all know their revenue. They just don't know what it produces. And here's the layer that makes it more complicated: many of them have been told what it means. They have advisors, accountants, dashboards with interpretations baked in. But those interpretations belong to someone else.

Two founders can have identical revenue and make completely different decisions, not because the numbers are different, but because their lens is.

> *"Revenue doesn't create clarity. Ownership of what it means does."*

* * *

Most founders treat revenue like a result. A signal that something is working. A number that represents progress.

But revenue doesn't answer the questions they're actually asking. It doesn't tell you what you can take home. What your business can sustain. What decisions are supported.

So when you rely on it, you end up trying to extract meaning from something that doesn't provide it.

The blind spot is this: you're treating revenue like clarity, when it's actually just input.

* * *

Revenue is not the outcome. It's the starting point.

It's the raw material your business generates. But raw material doesn't tell you what you can build. It has to be processed. Translated. Understood. And that understanding has to belong to you, not to whoever is in the room explaining it.

Most founders go from revenue directly to decision, without stopping at translation. And without that middle step, everything feels uncertain. Because you're making decisions from incomplete information, filtered through someone else's interpretation.

* * *

REVENUE → (External Interpretation) → Generic Decision

VERSUS

REVENUE → (Your Interpretation) → Aligned Decision

* * *

Here is what revenue needs to become before it's usable and before it's yours.

The first question is: what does the business keep? Revenue comes in, but not all of it stays. After cost of delivery, operating expenses, tools, systems and support, what is left after the business runs? Not theoretically. Actually. Because this is where many founders realize the number they've been celebrating is not the number they're working with.

The second question is: what does the owner earn? Not what's possible. Not what's left over. What is intentionally paid. I've seen founders generating strong revenue who are still unsure how much they're allowed to take. So they wait. They guess. They adjust month to month. And that uncertainty carries into everything else.

The third question is: what can the business support? This is where decisions start to connect. Can I hire? Can I invest? Can I expand? Not based on revenue, based on what remains after everything is accounted for. This is where clarity turns into action.

I once walked a founder through this step by step. We took her revenue and translated it, line by line. What it cost to operate. What was actually profit. What she was paying herself. When we finished, she sat back and said: "I've been making decisions off the wrong number this entire time."

Not because she didn't have the information. Because no one had ever connected it and she had never been taught to connect it herself.

* * *

You are not someone who tracks revenue to feel successful.

You are someone who understands what revenue creates and who owns that understanding.

That's the difference. Because once you see what your business actually produces, through your own lens, you stop chasing numbers for validation. And start using them for direction.

* * *

Revenue doesn't tell you how your business is doing.

It tells you where to start looking.

CHAPTER 11

Founder Pay Alignment

The way you pay yourself is the clearest reflection of how you see your role in your own business.

There's a moment that happens in almost every conversation I have with a founder.

It doesn't come at the beginning. It comes after we've talked about revenue. After we've walked through expenses. After everything feels like it's starting to make sense.

Then I ask one question: "How much do you pay yourself?"

And everything shifts. Not dramatically. Subtly. Their tone changes. Their posture adjusts. There's a pause that wasn't there before.

Sometimes the answer comes quickly, but it's followed by an explanation.

"Well, it depends." "I take what's left." "I reinvest most of it right now."

Other times, there's a longer silence. And then: "I don't really have a set number."

And that moment, right there, tells me more about the business than almost anything else we've discussed.

Because founder pay is never just about money. It's about how they see themselves in the business. How they prioritize stability. How decisions are being made behind the scenes.

I've seen founders building businesses that look successful from the outside, while quietly underpaying themselves. Waiting for a future version of the business to "earn" their compensation. Pushing their own stability to the side in the name of growth.

I remember working with a founder who had built something impressive. Consistent revenue. Strong client base. Clear demand. From the outside, everything looked solid. But as we walked through her numbers, something stood out.

Her business was functioning. She wasn't.

She had structured everything to support the business, but nothing to support herself. Her pay changed month to month. Sometimes she took more. Sometimes she took nothing. Depending on what felt "responsible" at the time.

At one point she said: "I just want to make sure the business is okay first."

And I understood what she meant. Because it sounds logical. Responsible. Even admirable. But there was something underneath it. A belief that the business deserves stability. The owner can wait.

And that belief, while common, is what creates long-term instability.

* * *

Most founders think of their pay as flexible. Something that adjusts based on what's happening in the business. So they treat it like a leftover. A reward. Something to figure out later. Instead of what it actually is: a core financial decision.

Because when your pay is unclear, everything connected to it becomes unclear. Your lifestyle. Your financial confidence. Your ability to make decisions.

The blind spot is this: you are treating your compensation like an outcome, instead of designing it as a structure.

* * *

Your business cannot be financially clear, if it cannot pay you correctly. Not eventually. Not someday. Now.

Because founder pay is not separate from the business. It is part of the system. And when that part of the system is unstable, it creates ripple effects everywhere else. You hesitate on decisions. You question your numbers. You feel pressure even when revenue is strong.

Not because something is wrong, but because something is misaligned.

* * *

Founder pay is not what's left over. It is a decision that must be defined.

And that decision should answer three things.

First: what does the business support? Before anything else, your pay must be grounded in reality, not what you want to take, but what the business can sustainably support. This connects directly to profit, cost structure and operational needs. Because your compensation cannot exist in isolation. It has to be integrated into the system.

Second: what does the owner need? This is where most founders disconnect. They don't clearly define what their household requires. What stability looks like personally. What consistency they need. So they operate in uncertainty, adjusting month to month instead of building something reliable.

Third: how does this scale? Your pay should not be random. It should evolve with your business. That means setting a baseline, defining how it increases and aligning it with growth. So as your business grows, you grow with it. Not behind it.

I once walked a founder through this in real time. We looked at her numbers. Defined what the business could support. Mapped what she actually needed. And set a clear structure for her pay. Nothing extreme. Nothing unrealistic. Just intentional.

She looked at me and said: "I've never paid myself like this before." Not because she couldn't. Because she had never decided to.

* * *

You are not someone who waits to be paid when the business allows it.

You are someone who builds a business that supports you intentionally.

That shift changes everything. Because now your decisions become clearer. Your confidence becomes grounded. Your business becomes aligned, not around growth alone, but around sustainability.

* * *

If your business doesn't know how to pay you, it doesn't know how to support you.

CHAPTER 12

Cost Structure Awareness

Your expenses are telling you the truth about your business, whether you're looking at them or not.

There's a moment that happens quietly in growing businesses.

No announcement. No clear signal. Just a gradual shift.

Revenue increases. So naturally, things expand. You invest in better tools. You bring on support. You upgrade systems. You say yes to things that feel like the next level. And none of it feels excessive. In fact, it feels justified. Responsible, even. Because growth requires support.

So you build. Layer by layer. Decision by decision.

Until one day, you notice something that doesn't quite make sense. You're making more. But it doesn't feel like you have more room. Not financially. Not mentally. Things feel tighter than they should. Decisions take longer. Spending feels heavier. And you can't quite point to one thing that caused it.

Because it wasn't one thing. It was everything, added slowly.

I remember sitting with a founder who was trying to understand why her business felt harder than it did the year before. Her revenue had grown. Her client base had expanded. On paper, everything pointed to progress.

But she kept saying: "I don't know why this feels so tight."

So we pulled everything up. Not just her revenue. Everything. Every expense. Every subscription. Every contractor. Every recurring cost. And we laid it out, line by line.

At first, nothing stood out. Everything had a reason. Everything had a purpose. But as we kept going, a pattern started to emerge. There was no single problem. There was accumulation. Small decisions made over time, without a clear view of their combined weight.

At one point she stopped and said: "I didn't realize how much I was carrying."

And that's the moment this becomes clear for most people. Not when something breaks. But when they finally see it.

* * *

Most founders don't intentionally overspend. What they do is say yes to things that make sense in the moment.

This tool will help. This person will save time. This investment will support growth.

And individually, those decisions are rarely wrong. But without structure, they stack. Quietly.

The blind spot is this: you're evaluating expenses individually, instead of understanding their collective impact. And what feels manageable in isolation can become heavy in total.

* * *

Your cost structure is not just a list of expenses. It's a reflection of how your business operates.

It tells you what your business depends on. How efficiently it runs. How much pressure it carries. And when that structure is unclear, growth doesn't create freedom. It creates weight. Because every dollar coming in already has somewhere to go, not intentionally, but by default.

And default decisions are rarely optimized.

* * *

Your expenses are not the problem. Your awareness of them determines whether they create pressure or support.

To understand your cost structure, you need to look at it through three lenses.

The first is fixed versus flexible. Not all expenses behave the same way. Some stay consistent regardless of revenue. Others scale with growth. If you don't know the difference, you can't predict how your business will respond as it grows.

The second is visible versus invisible. Some expenses are obvious, you see them every month. Others fade into the background: subscriptions, auto-renewals, small recurring charges. Individually, they don't feel significant. Collectively, they matter.

The third and most important, is support versus strain. Every expense either supports your capacity or adds pressure to maintain. Not all growth-related spending creates leverage. Some of it just increases responsibility.

Instead of asking "is this expense okay?", ask: "what is this expense doing to my business?" Is it increasing capacity? Is it reducing time? Is it improving outcomes? Or is it just sitting there, requiring revenue to sustain it?

After mapping everything out, that same founder made a simple adjustment. Not a massive cut. Not a drastic change. Just a few decisions, based on clarity instead of assumption. Within weeks, she said: "It finally feels like I have room again."

Not because she made more money. Because she understood what was already there.

* * *

You are not someone who manages expenses as they come.

You are someone who understands the structure those expenses create.

Because your business is not defined by how much it earns, but by how it operates underneath that revenue. And once you see that clearly, you stop reacting to pressure. And start designing for capacity.

* * *

Your business isn't heavy because of how much it costs.

It's heavy because of how little of that cost has been understood.

CHAPTER 13

Decision Timing

> *Most financial mistakes aren't bad decisions. They're decisions made at the wrong time.*

I was talking to a founder who had just hired someone she had been thinking about bringing on for months. On paper, it made sense. She was busy. Demand was there. She needed support. So she made the move.

But a few weeks in, something felt off. Not with the person. With the pressure. Her revenue hadn't caught up to the commitment yet. So instead of the hire creating relief, it created weight. Every month, there was a new question: "Can I sustain this?" Not because the decision was wrong. Because it was early.

On the other side, I've seen founders do the opposite. They know they need help. They feel it every day. Their time is stretched. Their capacity is limited. Opportunities are starting to slip. But they wait.

"I just need a little more consistency." "I'll do it after this next month." "I want to be sure."

So they hold. And hold. And hold. Until the cost of waiting becomes bigger than the cost of the decision. Missed opportunities. Delayed growth. Burnout that starts to affect how they show up. Not because hiring was wrong. Because waiting was.

Then there's the founder who invests at the right time, but without the structure to support it. They join the program. Make the investment. Commit to the next level. And for a moment, it feels like momentum. But behind the scenes, nothing else has shifted. No change in pricing. No adjustment in capacity. No space created to implement. So the investment sits. Not fully used. Not fully integrated. And instead of creating growth, it creates pressure. Not because the investment was wrong. Because it wasn't supported.

And then there's the quieter version. The founder who has the capacity to move, but doesn't. The money is there. The opportunity makes sense. But something holds them back. They wait for certainty. For the right moment. For the feeling that it's safe. Not realizing that sometimes the cost isn't in what you do, it's in what you delay.

* * *

Most founders evaluate decisions based on quality. "Is this a good idea?" "Does this make sense?" "Is this the right move?"

But that's only part of the equation. Because a good decision at the wrong time creates pressure. And a challenging decision at the right time creates momentum.

The blind spot is this: you're focused on what to do, without evaluating when it should happen.

* * *

Timing is what turns decisions into outcomes.

The same decision can create relief, stress, growth, or stagnation, depending on when it's made. So when something doesn't work, it's easy to question the decision itself. When the reality is: the decision may have been right. The timing wasn't.

Here's why we get timing wrong. Not because we don't care. Not because we're not capable. Because of how we process risk.

We move early to escape pressure. When things feel heavy, we want relief. So we act. We hire. We invest. We expand. Not from clarity, but from a desire to remove discomfort.

We delay to avoid risk. When decisions feel uncertain, we wait. We tell ourselves we're being responsible. But often we're trying to avoid making the wrong move, feeling exposed, or taking on something we can't fully control.

And there's a third factor that borrowed clarity makes worse: when you don't own your interpretation, you hesitate, or you move too early, not based on your read of the situation, but based on your level of trust in whoever told you it was time.

"Unclear ownership creates delayed decisions."

* * *

Timing is determined by support, not feeling. And not by someone else's recommendation alone.

A decision is well-timed when it is financially supported: can the business sustain this, not just now, but consistently? When it is operationally supported: do you have the capacity, structure, or systems to absorb this decision? And when it is strategically aligned: does this move connect to where you're going, or is it reacting to where you are?

Before making a decision, ask: what supports this right now? What pressure does this remove, or create? What changes if I wait? And, do I understand the answer to those questions from my own reading of the business, or from what I've been told?

That's how timing becomes intentional.

I once asked a founder: "If you make this decision today, what supports it?" She paused. Looked at her numbers. Then said: "Nothing yet."

And that answer changed everything. Not because the decision was wrong. Because it wasn't time. And she knew it, not because someone told her, but because she could see it.

* * *

NO OWNERSHIP → DOUBT → DELAY → MISSED OPPORTUNITY

or

NO OWNERSHIP → BLIND TRUST → EARLY ACTION → PRESSURE

* * *

You are not someone trying to make perfect decisions.

You are someone who understands when a decision is supported and who trusts your own read of that answer.

That's what creates momentum. Not guessing. Not waiting. Not reacting. But moving, with clarity behind you. Clarity that belongs to you.

* * *

It's not about making better decisions.

It's about making them at the right time, from the right understanding.

CHAPTER 14

Integration

> *Your business doesn't exist separately from your life. It funds it. It affects it. It shapes it. And if those two aren't aligned, you will feel it.*

There's a conversation I've had more times than I can count. It usually doesn't start with numbers. It starts with something that feels personal.

"I just want things to feel more stable." "I don't want to feel like I'm always guessing." "I want to know I'm okay, without constantly checking."

They're not asking about revenue. They're asking about how their life feels.

So we start looking at the business. The numbers are there. Revenue is coming in. Expenses are accounted for. From a distance, it looks functional. But as we go deeper, something becomes clear.

The business is making money. But it's not translating into a life that feels supported.

There's tension between what the business generates and what the person actually experiences. And that tension shows up everywhere. In decisions. In spending. In how they show up day to day. Not because something is broken. Because something isn't connected.

I remember working with a founder who had just had one of her best months. Strong revenue. Consistent clients. Everything moving. And yet, she hesitated over something small. A personal expense. Not large. Not unreasonable. Just something she wanted to do.

She paused and said: "I should probably wait." Not because she couldn't afford it. Because she didn't feel clear enough to say yes.

That moment always stands out to me. Because it shows the disconnect perfectly. The business was working. But her relationship to it wasn't. And that's what integration actually reveals.

* * *

Most founders operate as if their business and personal finances are separate. Business equals revenue, expenses, growth. Personal equals lifestyle, spending, stability. So they manage them independently.

But hope is not a system.

The blind spot is this: you're building a business without clearly connecting it to the life it's meant to support. And when that connection is missing, success feels incomplete.

* * *

Your business is not just a vehicle for revenue. It's a system that should support your life.

That means your income should be intentional. Your decisions should reflect your personal reality. And your growth should align with your capacity to live it.

Because if your business grows, but your life doesn't feel supported, something is misaligned. Not externally. Internally.

* * *

Financial clarity is not complete until your business and your life are connected.

That requires alignment in three areas.

The first is income to lifestyle alignment. Your business should produce income that supports your actual life, not a future version, not an ideal scenario. Your real, current needs. That means you know what your household requires. What stability looks like personally. What consistency you need to feel grounded. Without this, you're building without a target.

The second is decisions to life impact awareness. Every business decision has a personal impact. Hiring affects your time. Spending affects your flexibility. Growth affects your capacity. So decisions should not just be evaluated by "does this help the business?" but also "what does this do to my life?"

The third is growth to capacity alignment. Growth should not outpace your ability to live it. Because when it does, you experience more stress, less presence and reduced clarity. Not because growth is wrong. Because it's unsupported.

Instead of asking "how do I grow this business?", ask: "how do I grow this business in a way that supports my life?" That question changes your decisions completely.

After walking through this with a founder, she paused and said: "I've been building something that looks successful, but doesn't feel supportive." And then: "I don't want that anymore."

That's the moment integration begins. Not with numbers. With a decision.

* * *

When your business and your life are aligned, everything changes.

Decisions become clearer because they're grounded in something real. Money feels different because it has direction. Growth feels different because it's sustainable.

You stop asking "is this working?" and start experiencing "this supports me."

That's what financial clarity actually creates. Not just better numbers. Better alignment.

* * *

You are not someone building a business for the sake of growth.

You are someone designing a business that supports the way you want to live.

That's a different standard. A higher one. Because now your decisions are intentional, your structure is aligned and your outcomes are connected.

And that's where clarity becomes power.

* * *

If your business doesn't support your life, it's not finished.

Act IV

THE
TRANSFORMATION

CHAPTER 15

Financial Range of Motion

The goal isn't to make more money. It's to have more options.

There's a moment that doesn't get talked about enough.

Not the breakthrough. Not the big revenue milestone. Something quieter. More subtle.

A founder is reviewing her numbers. Not rushing. Not guessing. Not trying to piece things together. Just, looking. And understanding.

She knows what came in. Where it went. What's available. What decisions are supported. There's no tension in the process. No second-guessing. No need to check the same number multiple times.

Just clarity. And from that clarity, something shifts. She makes a decision. Not hesitantly. Not reactively. Directly. Because she can see it.

That moment doesn't look dramatic from the outside. But internally, it's everything. Because for the first time, the decision doesn't feel like risk. It feels like direction.

I've also seen the opposite. A founder in the same position, reviewing the same types of numbers, but the experience is completely different. They open everything. Scan quickly. Pause. Recheck. Try to piece together what's actually happening.

"Can I do this?" "Should I wait?" "Is this too much?"

The information is there. But the clarity isn't. So every decision feels heavier than it needs to. Not because the business is unstable. Because it's unclear.

And that difference, between those two experiences, is what most people are actually chasing. Not just growth. Not just income. But the ability to move without hesitation.

* * *

Most founders think they want more money. And on the surface, that's true.

But what they actually want is what they believe more money will give them: flexibility. Confidence. The ability to decide.

So they focus on increasing revenue, hoping it will create those outcomes.

But without clarity, more money doesn't create more options. It creates more responsibility.

The blind spot is this: you're chasing income when what you actually want is flexibility.

* * *

Flexibility doesn't come from how much you make. It comes from how clearly you understand what you can do, from a lens that is yours.

That's what creates faster decisions, reduced hesitation and real confidence. Because options are only useful if you know which ones are available. And clarity, your own clarity, not borrowed, is what makes that visible.

* * *

Financial clarity creates range of motion.

Range of motion means you are not locked into one way of operating. You have options. And you can act on them.

What does range of motion look like in practice? It looks like knowing when you can hire, without second-guessing. Making an investment, without destabilizing everything else. Paying yourself consistently, without guilt or confusion. Decisions that used to take days, taking minutes. Not because you're rushing. Because you can see.

What does range of motion feel like internally? It feels like calm instead of tension. Certainty instead of guessing. Movement instead of hesitation. You're no longer asking "am I okay?" You know.

What does range of motion enable? This is where it changes everything. Because once clarity is in place, your options expand. You can say yes faster. Say no confidently. Adjust without panic. Move without overthinking. And that doesn't just affect your business. It affects how you experience it.

I once asked a founder after we had worked through her numbers: "How do decisions feel different now?"

She didn't talk about money. She said: "I don't feel stuck anymore."

That's range of motion. Not just having options. Being able to move.

* * *

When you have financial range of motion, growth feels different. It's not something you chase. It's something you choose.

Because now you understand what supports expansion. You know when to move. You trust your decisions, because they come from your understanding, not someone else's.

Opportunities don't feel overwhelming. They feel available. And instead of reacting to what's happening, you start directing where things go.

That's when your business shifts. From something you manage, to something you lead.

* * *

You are not someone trying to create stability by making more money.

You are someone who creates flexibility through clarity, clarity that belongs to you.

That's a higher level of operation. Because now your decisions are faster, your confidence is grounded and your growth is intentional.

And that's what creates real freedom.

* * *

Freedom isn't found in your revenue.

It's found in your ability to move.

CHAPTER 16

The New Standard

At some point, clarity stops being something you learn and becomes something you require.

There's a moment that happens after everything starts to click.

Not all at once. But enough. Enough understanding. Enough visibility. Enough decisions made from clarity instead of reaction.

And things begin to feel different. Not easier, cleaner. You look at your numbers and you understand them. You make decisions and you don't second-guess them. You move and it feels supported.

And then something subtle happens. You try to go back. Back to how you used to operate. Quick checks. Rough estimates. "Good enough" decisions. And it doesn't sit right anymore.

Not because you've become rigid. Because your standard has changed.

I've seen this with founders who once avoided their numbers and now refuse to make a move without understanding them. Not out of fear. Out of expectation.

But there's a specific version of this that matters most. It's not just that you require clarity now. It's that you require your own clarity. You've stopped accepting explanations at face value. You've stopped moving without understanding. You've stopped deferring decisions by default.

You now require interpretation. Alignment. Ownership. And that's a different standard than most founders ever reach.

* * *

Most people think growth is about doing more. More effort. More strategy. More execution. So they focus on increasing capacity. But they don't raise their standards.

They tolerate unclear numbers. Delayed decisions. Reactive thinking. And borrowed clarity, because it's familiar. Because it used to feel like enough.

The blind spot is this: you're trying to grow your results without upgrading the standard you operate by. And growth without a higher standard creates inconsistency.

* * *

The next level of your business is not created by new tactics. It's created by new standards.

What you tolerate. What you require. What you refuse to operate without.

Because your standards determine how you make decisions, how quickly you move and how stable your outcomes are. And ownership, not just clarity, but ownership of how you interpret and decide, is one of those standards.

"Clarity is not a luxury. It's a standard."

* * *

Here is what the new standard looks like, not in theory, but in practice.

I don't make decisions without clarity. No more "I think this makes sense" or "this should work." If it's not clear, it's not decided.

> *"If it's not clear, it's not a yes."*

I know what my numbers mean, not just what they are. It's not enough to see revenue, check balances, or review reports. You understand what your business produces, what it supports and what decisions are available.

> *"Numbers don't create clarity. Interpretation does."*

I pay myself with intention. No more leftovers. No more guessing. No more inconsistent withdrawals. Your pay is defined, supported and aligned. Because you are not separate from the business. You are part of it.

> *"If the business works, but you don't, it's not working."*

I understand what my business requires to operate. No more surprise expenses, quiet accumulation, or hidden pressure. You know what it costs to run, what increases with growth and what creates strain versus support.

> *"Everything in your business has a cost. Clarity tells you if it's worth it."*

I move when decisions are supported, not when they feel urgent. No more reactive hiring. No more delayed action. No more emotionally driven moves. You evaluate timing, support and alignment and you move accordingly.

> *"Urgency is not a signal. Clarity is."*

My business supports my life, not competes with it. No more disconnect between income and lifestyle. No more success that feels heavy. No more growth without alignment. Everything connects. Everything supports.

> *"If your business doesn't support your life, it's not done."*

And the standard that holds all others together: if it's not my interpretation, it's not my decision. You no longer accept someone else's lens as your own. You evaluate. You pressure-test. You align every recommendation with your own understanding. And then you decide.

> *"If it's not your interpretation, it's not your decision."*

* * *

OLD STANDARD: REPORT → TRUST → ACTION

NEW STANDARD: REPORT → UNDERSTAND → INTERPRET → DECIDE

* * *

Take a moment and consider this.

Where are you still tolerating confusion? Where are you still making decisions from assumption, urgency, or incomplete information? Where are you still accepting borrowed clarity, because it feels easier than building your own?

Because once you see what's possible, you have a choice. To go back. Or to raise the standard.

You are not someone trying to improve your business.

You are someone who operates at a higher standard. A standard where clarity is required, decisions are supported and structure replaces guessing and where the interpretation that drives your decisions is yours.

That standard changes everything. Because now you don't chase confidence, you operate from it. You don't wait for stability, you create it. You don't react to growth, you lead it.

* * *

You don't need more to change your business.

You need a higher standard for how you operate within it.

> *"The results you want are on the other side of the standards you haven't set yet."*

CHAPTER 17

Clarity Before Crisis

> *Most businesses don't fail because something went wrong. They fail because something wasn't seen early enough.*

I remember a conversation that didn't start with strategy. It started with urgency.

"Something's off."

That's all she said. No specifics. No clear issue. Just a feeling.

Revenue hadn't dropped dramatically. Nothing had broken overnight. But something didn't feel right.

So we started looking. Not quickly. Not reactively. Carefully. And what we found wasn't one problem. It was a series of things that had been building quietly: expenses that had increased gradually, decisions made without full visibility, assumptions that had never been confirmed.

Nothing extreme on its own. But together, they had created pressure that hadn't been recognized yet. And the only reason it was being felt now was because something finally forced it to the surface. Not because it had just started. Because it had been there.

I've also seen the opposite. A founder reviewing her numbers, not because something was wrong, but because it was part of how she operated. She noticed a small shift. Not dramatic. Just different. And because she understood what she was looking at, through her own lens, she adjusted early. Before it became pressure. Before it became stress. Before it became a problem.

Same type of business. Same level of complexity. Different outcome.

Not because one was better. Because one had clarity earlier. And because that clarity was hers, she could see what was changing without waiting for someone else to tell her.

* * *

Most founders don't think about prevention. They think about response.

When something feels off: look, adjust, react. Because that's how most things are taught. Fix what's broken. But by the time something feels broken, it's already been building.

The blind spot is this: you're waiting for pressure to tell you there's a problem, instead of using clarity to see it before it forms.

* * *

Clarity is not just for understanding where you are. It's for protecting where you're going.

Because when you can see clearly and when that clarity belongs to you, you don't wait for problems to become visible. You catch them early. When they're still small. When they're still manageable. When they don't carry weight yet.

That's what separates reactive businesses from stable ones. Not effort. Not intelligence. Timing of awareness and ownership of what you're seeing.

> *"Crisis doesn't create problems. It exposes what was already unclear."*

* * *

Clarity is preventative. It allows you to do three things.

Detect shifts early. You notice changes in revenue patterns, increases in cost and pressure building before it's obvious. Not because someone flagged it for you, because you're looking, you understand what you're seeing and you've built the habit of looking.

Adjust before it hurts. You don't wait until decisions feel urgent. You move while you still have options. Because you saw the shift before it became a crisis.

Maintain stability through growth. As your business expands, your clarity expands with it. So growth doesn't introduce risk. It reveals opportunity. Because you're equipped to see it clearly.

Instead of asking "what do I do when something goes wrong?", ask: "what can I see now, before it becomes a problem?" That's a different level of operation.

I once asked a founder: "When was the first moment this started to feel off?" She paused. Then said: "A while ago, I just didn't look at it then."

That's the gap. Not between failure and success. Between seeing and waiting.

* * *

You are not someone who waits for problems to show up.

You are someone who sees early and moves early.

That's what creates stability. Not reacting faster. Seeing sooner. And trusting what you see because the interpretation is yours.

* * *

The goal is not to fix problems faster.

It's to see them before they exist.

> *"Clarity before crisis is what keeps your business from becoming the lesson."*

CHAPTER 18

You Were Never Bad With Money

> *You were never bad with money. You were working with information that didn't make sense, interpreted through someone else's lens.*

I've had this conversation at the end of many client engagements.

After everything has been mapped out. After the numbers make sense. After decisions feel clear.

There's a moment where they look at everything and then look back at me. And say something like: "I can't believe I didn't see this before."

And I always pause. Because that sentence carries something deeper than realization. It carries judgment. On themselves. For something they were never actually equipped to see.

So I ask them a different question: "What were you using before this?"

And the answer is always the same. Instinct. Guessing. What they were told. What they could piece together.

They weren't operating without effort. They were operating without translation and without a lens that belonged to them.

I think about how many founders sit in that space before clarity. Working hard. Trying to be responsible. Making decisions the best way they know how. And quietly believing:

"I should be better at this." "I should understand this more." "I shouldn't feel this confused."

So they carry it. The uncertainty. The hesitation. The pressure. Not just operationally, personally.

And that's the part that needs to be addressed directly. Because this was never about ability.

* * *

Most people internalize financial confusion. They make it mean something about them.

"I'm not good with numbers." "I need someone else to handle this." "I'll never fully understand it."

So they disconnect. They avoid. They delegate without clarity. They stay removed from the one thing that shapes everything else.

But here is the truth beneath that belief: they didn't disconnect because they were incapable. They disconnected because the interpretation was always someone else's. Because no one built them a system that made their own numbers accessible to them. Because borrowed clarity felt safer than no clarity at all.

The blind spot is this: you've turned a lack of clarity into a personal limitation, when what you actually lacked was ownership.

* * *

You were never bad with money.

You were never given a system that made it usable and no one taught you to build a lens of your own.

That's it. Because once the information changes and once the interpretation becomes yours, your behavior changes. Your confidence changes. Your decisions change.

Not because you became someone new. Because you were finally working with something that made sense. Something that belonged to you.

* * *

Everything in this book comes back to one thing: clarity creates capability. But not just any clarity. Your clarity. The kind that doesn't disappear when the meeting ends, when the advisor leaves, or when the report stops making sense.

When you can see what your business produces, through your own understanding and make decisions from that place, you don't need more motivation, more discipline, or more effort.

You need the right interpretation. And you need it to be yours.

—

You are not someone trying to get better with money.

You are someone who understands it. Who can read it. Use it. Move with it.

You were not incapable. You were not irresponsible. You were not behind.

You were interpreting through someone else's lens. Deciding without ownership. Moving without a framework of your own.

That changes now.

* * *

Nothing about you needed to change.

Only what you were working with and who it belonged to.

> *"You were never behind. You were just working without clarity."*

And now you're not.

* * *

> **BEFORE:**
> OUTSIDE INTERPRETATION → DECISION → UNCERTAINTY
>
> **AFTER:**
> OWNED INTERPRETATION → DECISION → CONFIDENCE

CHAPTER 19

The Decision You Make Now

> *This is the chapter most books don't write. Not because there's nothing left to say. But because what comes next isn't something I can do for you.*

You've moved through the illusion, the belief that more revenue, a growing business and a trusted advisor meant you were in control.

You've sat with the reframe, the recognition that the problem was never the money. It was the clarity. And more specifically, it was the ownership of that clarity.

You've walked through the system, the five decisions that determine whether your revenue actually improves your life. Revenue reality. Founder pay. Cost structure. Decision timing. Integration.

And you've seen what becomes possible on the other side: range of motion. A higher standard. The ability to see problems before they become crises. The understanding that you were never bad with money, you were just working without a lens of your own.

Now comes the part that matters most.

What do you do with this?

* * *

There are two responses to everything you've read in this book.

The first response is relief. The recognition that what you've been experiencing, the confusion, the hesitation, the quiet sense that something was off even when everything looked right, wasn't a character flaw. It wasn't incompetence. It was the natural result of operating without a decision system that belonged to you.

That relief is real. And it matters.

But relief is not a plan.

The second response is the one that changes your business. It's the decision to stop borrowing someone else's clarity and to start building your own.

Not to replace your advisors. Not to become your own accountant. But to become the owner of the lens through which your business is seen and your decisions are made.

That decision is not a one-time event. It's a standard. And like every standard, it has to be chosen, repeatedly, intentionally, in the moments when it's easier to defer, to agree, to hand it over and trust that someone else has it handled.

* * *

Here is what I know about the founders who make that shift.

They don't become perfect at finances. They don't stop needing support. They don't suddenly find it all simple.

What changes is what happens in the room. When the advisor presents a recommendation, they ask what it means, not just whether it sounds right. When the report shows a number, they understand what it represents, not just whether it's higher than last month. When a decision arrives, they evaluate it from their own reading of the business, not from deference to someone else's authority.

They become, in the truest sense, the decision architect of their own business.

That's not a credential. It's a posture. And it's available to every founder who chooses it.

* * *

If you're ready to move from borrowed clarity to owned clarity, here is where to start.

Start with revenue reality. Before anything else, answer this: what does your revenue actually produce? Not what it represents. Not what it signals. What does it turn into, in profit, in owner pay, in operating capacity? If you can't answer that question from your own understanding, that's your starting point.

Then move to your pay. Define it. Not what's left over. Not what feels responsible. What the business can support, what you actually need and how those two connect.

Then look at your cost structure, not as a list of expenses, but as a map of how your business operates. What's fixed. What's flexible. What's supporting capacity and what's creating strain.

Then build timing into your decision process. Before you move on anything significant, ask what supports it right now, financially, operationally and strategically. And ask whether your answer comes from your own reading of the situation or from what you've been told.

Finally, integrate. Make sure your business and your life are connected. That what you're building serves the way you want to live. That success and support are the same thing, not competing forces.

That's the Niacin Clarity Framework. Five decisions. Repeated consistently. Owned completely.

* * *

One last thing.

The founders who stay stuck, not because they don't understand that something needs to change, but because they wait for the perfect moment, the right conditions, the certainty that it's time, are making a decision too.

They're deciding to keep borrowing.

And borrowed clarity has a cost. It compounds, quietly, the same way financial misalignment does. Every month you operate without your own lens is a month your decisions are shaped by someone else's understanding of your business.

You've read this book. You understand the problem in a way you didn't before. And that means the question is no longer whether you can see it.

The question is what you do now that you can.

* * *

You were never behind. You were just working without clarity.

Now you have it. What you build with it is yours.

An Invitation

This book was designed to give you a framework. But a framework only works when it's used and the most powerful version of this work happens in context.

Your business is not generic. Your numbers tell a specific story. Your decisions carry specific weight. And the clarity you need is not one-size-fits-all, it's built around the structure of your business, the demands of your life and the decisions that are uniquely yours to make.

That's the work I do inside NIACIN Educators.

* * *

If you're ready to move from the concepts in this book to the application inside your actual business, here is where to go next.

The Financial Clarity Intensive is designed for founders who are ready to build their decision architecture from the ground up. We take the five decisions from this book and apply them directly to your numbers, your structure and your next moves. You leave with a financial decision system that belongs to you, not a report to file away, but a lens to operate from.

The Decision Architecture Advisory is for founders who are already generating consistent revenue and are ready to operate at the level this book describes, where clarity is not a project but a standard. We work together over time to build the systems, the visibility and the decision capacity that make borrowed clarity permanently unnecessary.

Both begin with a conversation. Because before any framework is built, I want to understand what you're actually working with, the real picture, not the surface numbers.

* * *

If that's where you are, the next step is simple.

Come find me at NiacinEducators.com. The work continues there.

* * *

And if this book found its way to you through a stage, a mastermind, or the hands of someone who thought you needed it, I hope it confirmed something you already suspected.

You were never the problem.

You were just working without the right tools.

Now you're not.

* * *

NIACIN Educators
Financial Decision Architecture for Founders
NiacinEducators.com